*Little Children's Bible Books*

# THE
# FIRST
# EASTER

BROADMAN
&HOLMAN
PUBLISHERS

*Retold by Anne de Graaf*

*Illustrated by José Pérez Montero*

# THE FIRST EASTER

Published in 2000 by Broadman & Holman Publishers,
Nashville, Tennessee

Text copyright © 2000 Anne de Graaf
Illustration copyright © 2000 José Pérez Montero
Design by Ben Alex
Conceived, designed and produced by Scandinavia Publishing House
Printed in Hong Kong
ISBN 0-8054-2188-2

*Dedicated to Pedro Pérez Rollán
and Channy Lyn Potter*

When Jesus entered Jerusalem, the people cheered for him in a parade. A parade just for Jesus! They waved palm branches up and down.

The church leaders did not like Jesus. They wanted to catch Jesus. They paid his disciple, Judas, thirty pieces of silver to help them.

*Look around you. Can you find thirty silver-colored things?*

Jesus thanked God in Jerusalem
with bread and wine. He broke
the bread into pieces, and passed
the bread and wine to his friends.

Jesus talked about dying and going to heaven. "I will make a place there for everyone. I am the Way. Don't be afraid. Someday I'll take you home to heaven."

*Do you know anyone Jesus has already taken home to heaven? Now say a prayer for the people that person left behind.*

13

Judas led Jesus' enemies right
to Jesus. But Peter fought
back! He cut off the ear of a
guard. Jesus teaches us to love
our enemies. He picked up the
ear and made it better.

*Rub the ear of the person reading to you. Now it's your turn!*

Peter was scared after the guards took Jesus away. They asked him, "You know Jesus, don't you?" But he said, "No, no, no!" Three times Peter lied about knowing Jesus. Then the rooster crowed.

*What did the rooster sound like?*

17

Jesus' enemies brought him before a judge. "Kill him on the cross!" they screamed.

But the judge said, "He's done nothing wrong."

The soldiers hurt Jesus.
His friends and family were
scared. His enemies nailed
him to the cross so he
would die.

*What terrible words Jesus' enemies said! I am going to hide in my cocoon. Just watch what happens!*

Jesus died so he could give all people who choose to believe in him, new life. Close your eyes and thank him now for that most special gift.

After Jesus died, his friends and family took him down off the cross. They were crying and very sad. They placed him gently in a special cave, with guards outside.

*This was such a dark time, as dark as the night. But what comes after the night?*

A few days later, Jesus' friends came back to the cave. It was empty! "Where is Jesus?" they cried. The guards didn't know anything.

*See if you can find signs of new life outside: a tiny tree, a flower, the morning sun.*

An angel said, "Look inside the cave. Jesus is alive again! He's not dead! Be happy! Go tell everyone that he's alive." The women ran off, hardly believing their eyes and ears.

31

Thomas would not believe that Jesus was alive again. Jesus said, "You believe in me because you see me. Those who believe without seeing are very, very special."

*That's you and me. Point to yourself and say, "Jesus thinks I'm special!"*

One spring morning, Jesus visited
his friends who were fishing and
said, "Throw your net out again!"
Then they caught so many fish,
the net almost burst!

Which season is Easter in? Not winter, autumn, or summer! SPRING! Spring is the time for baby lambs and butterflies!

After Jesus rose from the dead, he visited his friends many times. Once he said, "In heaven there are many rooms. I will get them ready for you." Then Jesus went to heaven.

How many rooms does your home have? Now name just as many signs of new life and thank God for each one of them.

## A NOTE TO THE big PEOPLE:

The *Little Children's Bible Books* may be your child's first introduction to the Bible, God's Word. This book about the first Easter makes the four Gospels spring to life. This is a DO book. Point things out and ask your child to find, seek, say, and discover.

Before you read these stories, pray that your child's little heart would be touched by the love of God. These stories are about planting seeds, having vision, learning right from wrong, and choosing to believe. Pray together after you read this. There's no better way for big people to learn from little people.

*A little something fun is said in italics by the narrating animal to make the story come alive. In this DO book, wave, wink, hop, roar, or do any of the other things the stories suggest so this can become a fun time of growing closer.*